NOPL @ CICERO
8686 KNOWLEDGE LN.
CICERO, NY 13039

Are You My Rodent?

by Marybeth Mataya
Illustrated by Matthew Williams

Content Consultant:
Gerald Brecke
Doctor of Veterinary Medicine

Are You My Pet?

visit us at www.abdopublishing.com

Published by Magic Wagon, a division of the ABDO Publishing Group, 8000 West 78th Street, Edina, Minnesota 55439. Copyright © 2009 by Abdo Consulting Group, Inc. International copyrights reserved in all countries. All rights reserved. No part of this book may be reproduced in any form without written permission from the publisher.

Looking Glass Library™ is a trademark and logo of Magic Wagon.

Printed in the United States.

Text by Marybeth Mataya
Illustrations by Matthew Williams
Edited by Jill Sherman
Interior layout and design by Emily Love
Cover design by Emily Love

Library of Congress Cataloging-in-Publication Data

Mataya, Marybeth.
 Are you my rodent? / by Marybeth Mataya ; illustrated by Matthew Williams ; content consultant, Gerald Brecke.
     p. cm. — (Are you my pet?)
 Includes index.
 ISBN 978-1-60270-246-2
 1. Rodents as pets—Juvenile literature. I. Williams, Matthew, 1971- ill. II. Title.
 SF459.R63M38 2009
 636.935—dc22

2008003647

Note to Parents/Guardians:
This book can help you teach your child how to be a kind, responsible pet owner. Even so, a child will not be able to handle all the responsibilities of having a pet, so we are glad that you will oversee the responsibility. Since diseases can be passed from animals to humans, veterinarians suggest that adults take care of droppings and clean cages or aquariums.

Table of Contents

Is a Rodent the Right Pet for Me?	4
What Kind of Rodent Would Be Best?	7
Where Should My Pet Live?	11
What Should I Feed My Pet?	17
What Else Does My Pet Need?	18
How Do I Get to Know My Pet?	22
How Do I Play with My Pet?	25
How Do I Keep My Pet Healthy?	26
Words to Know	30
Further Reading	31
On the Web	31
Index	32

Is a Rodent the Right Pet for Me?

Do you think small animals are cute? Do you want an indoor pet? Do you want to cuddle with someone furry?

Then a rodent may be the pet for you! Guinea pigs, hamsters, gerbils, mice, and rats are all rodents. Some people call these animals "pocket pets." To pick one, you need to know about each.

Pet Fact:
A rodent's front teeth will grow its whole life. A rodent needs to chew on things to keep its teeth short.

6

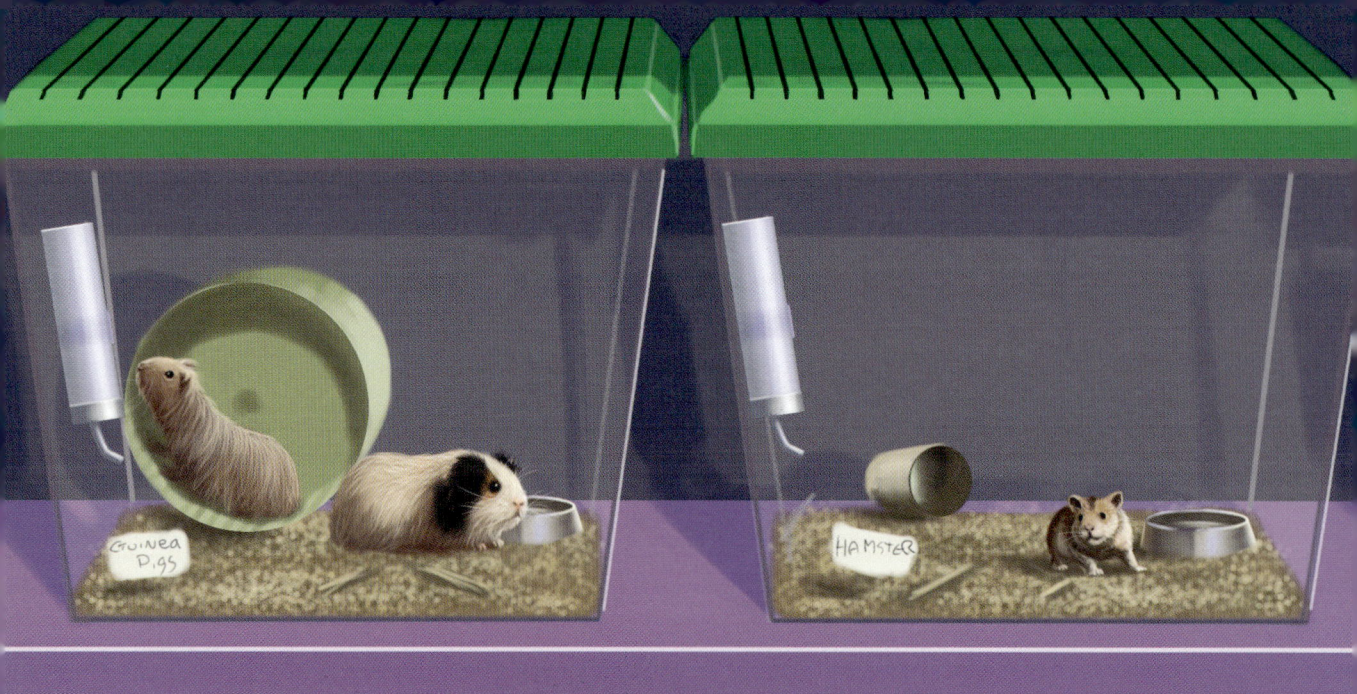

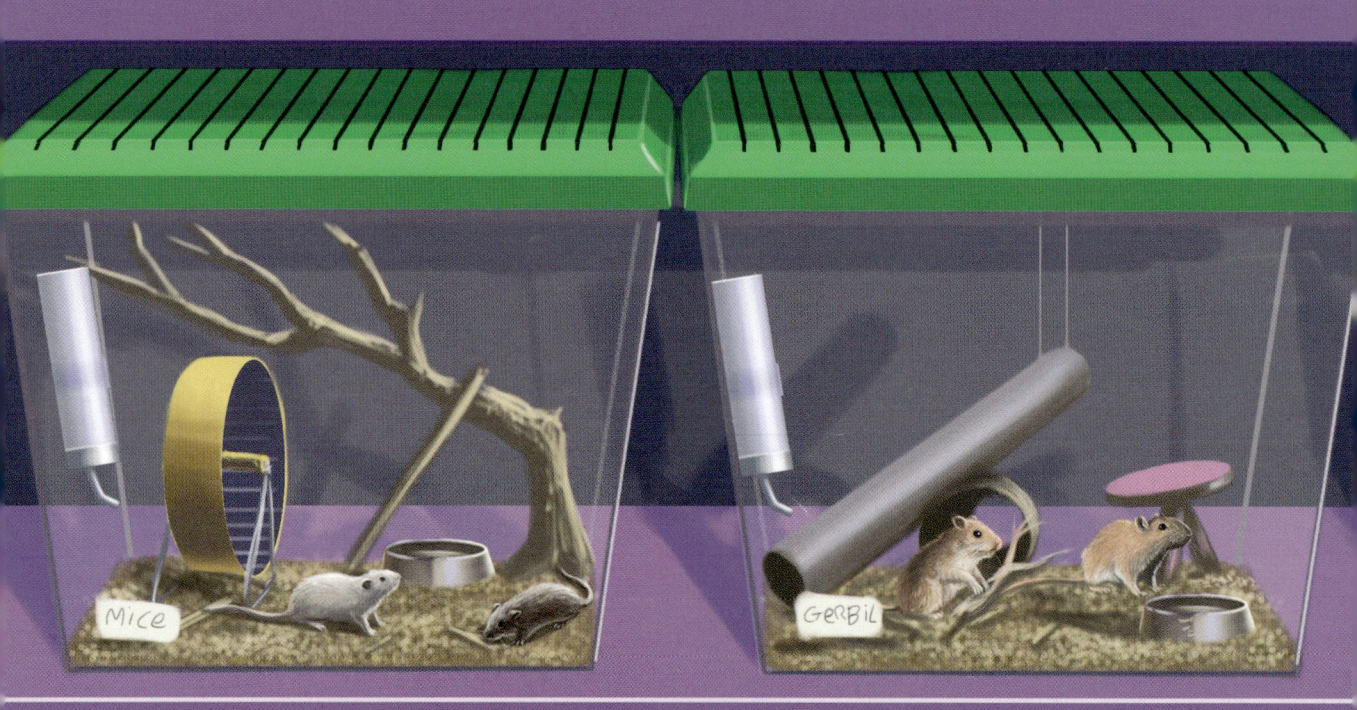

What Kind of Rodent Would Be Best?

Guinea pigs are pudgy and gentle. They are the biggest of the pocket pets. Their large tummies sway when they move. Guinea pigs may live from five to seven years.

Hamsters are round and friendly. They can be held easily. They have large cheeks to carry food. Hamsters may live from three to five years.

Gerbils are small with furry tails. They are friendly and fast-moving. They like to dig! Gerbils may live from three to five years.

Mice are tiny. They have long tails without fur. They are smart and fun to watch, but not to hold. They scare easily, pee often, and bite. Mice may live from one to three years.

Rats are medium-sized and soft. They have long hairless tails. They are easy to train and hold. Rats can become fond of the people who care for them. Rats may live from two to four years.

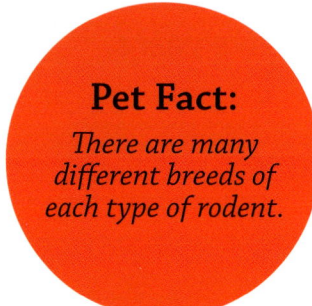

Pet Fact:
There are many different breeds of each type of rodent.

10

Where Should My Pet Live?

An aquarium is a good place for a rodent to live. It is a clear glass or plastic box. The sides of the box must be tall. You do not want your pet to get out. Allow enough room for your pet to run around. Cover the top with a wire screen, and keep it closed with a good latch. This lid will prevent your pet from escaping!

Your pet can also live in a wire cage. The spaces between the wires must be small so your pet cannot squeeze through.

Line the bottom of your pet's home with newspaper, then add bedding. Bedding can be made of thin bits of wood, shredded paper, or straw. Do not buy cedar or pine wood bedding. Your pet also needs a place to hide and sleep. Add an old flower pot or cardboard box with clean rags for a soft cloth bed.

Be careful about where you put your pet's home. It should not be cold, damp, hot, or stuffy. It should be quiet and not too bright.

Hamsters, mice, and rats are often awake at night. They can be loud. You may want to put them in a room with a door.

Pet Fact:
Hamsters whistle and grunt when they are excited. Guinea pigs chatter with their teeth. Rats squeak when they are scared and click their teeth when they are happy.

What Should I Feed My Pet?

Buy food packs for small rodents or for your kind of rodent. These pets also like seeds, fruit, and vegetables. Give them small pieces. Guinea pigs need hay and citrus fruits. A metal or clay bowl can hold your pet's food.

Hang a water bottle with a metal tube. Your pet needs fresh water every day.

Pet Fact:
Some foods make rodents sick. Chocolate, onions, candy, cabbage, corn, uncooked beans, peanuts, and rhubarb are bad for rodents.

What Else Does My Pet Need?

Hamsters like to live alone. But many rodents like company. If you have more than one animal, their home has to be large enough for all of them. Do not put a male and a female in the same home.

Pet Fact:
Rodents can chew through almost anything. They can pull things into their cage and chew them. Keep your things away from the cage!

Do not forget, your pet will need exercise! A wheel will work for most of these pets. Be sure the wheel does not have holes. Your pet's feet could get stuck.

Your rodent will also need something healthy to chew on, such as a twig or a branch.

How Do I Get to Know My Pet?

At first, you should leave your pet alone. It will want to get used to its new home. Then you can let it sniff your hand, so it can get to know you.

Later, you can pick up your pet and hold it. Remember to be gentle. Wear old clothes or place a rag on your lap. Hold your pet a few times each day.

Pet Fact:
Rodents have thin bones. They need to be scooped up so their bottoms are held. Never squeeze your pet! Never hold it by its tail!

How Do I Play with My Pet?

You can play with your pet in a box or a small closed room. Put a towel under the door so it will not escape. If your pet is napping, leave it alone. You do not want to make your pet cranky. Cranky pets may bite or scratch!

Pet Fact:
Rodents like to play with toys. They like tunnels and mazes. Give them toilet paper tubes or cardboard boxes with holes in them.

How Do I Keep My Pet Healthy?

Droppings, or poop, should be removed every day. Change the bedding and newspaper. Wash the aquarium or cage's floor every week. If your pet's home is clean, your pet will stay clean too! Wash your hands before and after you hold your pet or your pet's things.

27

If your pet is hurt, looks sad, or is not eating, take it to a veterinarian. This animal doctor will help you keep your pet healthy. The more you learn about your pet, the better you can care for it!

Pet Fact:

Rodents like to keep clean. They spend a lot of time grooming, or washing themselves.

Words to Know

aquarium—a tank to hold fish or other animals.

bedding—shredded paper or other material lining an animal cage.

breed—a specific kind of animal within a species.

droppings—animal poop.

veterinarian—an animal doctor.

Further Reading

Birmelin, Immanuel. *My Guinea Pig and Me*. Hauppauge, NY: Barron's Educational Series, 2001.
Holliman, Peter. *My Hamster and Me*. Hauppauge, NY: Barron's Educational Series, 2001.
Kotter, Engelbert. *My Gerbil and Me*. Hauppauge, NY: Barron's Educational Series, 2005.
Lange, Monika. *My Rat and Me*. Hauppauge, NY: Barron's Educational Series, 2005.
Leavitt, Amie Jane. *Care for a Pet Mouse*. Hockessin, DE: Mitchell Lane Publishers, 2007.

On the Web

To learn more about rodents, visit ABDO Publishing Company on the World Wide Web at **www.abdopublishing.com**. Web sites about rodents are featured on our Book Links page. These links are routinely monitored and updated to provide the most current information available.

Index

A
aquariums 11, 14, 26

B
bedding 12, 26
breeds 8

C
cages 12, 14, 18, 26
chattering 14
chewing 4, 18, 20
cleanup 26

D
digging 7
droppings 26

E
exercise 20

F
food 7, 17
fur 4, 7, 8

G
gerbil 4, 7
grooming 28
grunting 14
guinea pig 4, 7, 14, 17

H
hamster 4, 7, 14, 18
handling 22, 25, 26
hiding 12

L
lids 12
life span 7, 8

M
mouse 4, 8, 14

P
playing 25

R
rat 4, 8, 14

S
safety 26, 28
sickness 17, 28
size 4, 7, 8
squeaking 14

T
teeth 4, 14
toys 25

V
veterinarians 28

W
water 17
wheels 20
whistling 14